THE UNSEEN WAR:

My Encounter with faith and Darkness

Yvonne Bryant

WestBow
PRESS®
A DIVISION OF THOMAS NELSON
& ZONDERVAN

WestBow Press books may be ordered through booksellers or by contacting:

WestBow Press
A Division of Thomas Nelson & Zondervan
1663 Liberty Drive
Bloomington, IN 47403
www.westbowpress.com
844-714-3454

ISBN: 979-8-3850-3802-2 (sc)
ISBN: 979-8-3850-3801-5 (e)

Print information available on the last page.

WestBow Press rev. date: 11/21/2024

I dedicate this book to my Lord
and savior Jesus Christ.

TABLE OF CONTENTS

INTRODUCTION

I was born and raised in a small town in Africa. Life in those early years was full of love, wisdom, and guidance from my Grandma and Grandpa, who were pivotal in shaping my childhood. They instilled in me the values of faith, family, and resilience. However, everything changed when I turned twelve years old. My mother enrolled me in an all-girls school, and by the age of sixteen, I found myself in a completely different world—the United States. I completed high school in Chicago and went on to attend college in Rhode Island.

God has blessed me with three wonderful children: Derrick, Kayla, and John-Christian. I am married to Robert Bryant, and together we have built a life in a small town in North Carolina. Though my journey has taken me across continents and through various stages of life, one thing has remained constant: my connection to the church. I grew up in a household where faith was central, and our family faithfully attended the Episcopal Church.

However, it was not until I was twenty-eight that my relationship with God took a transformative turn. A workmate invited me to her church—a Baptist congregation—and it was there that I gave my life to Christ and was baptized. That moment marked the beginning of my spiritual journey, one filled with both discovery and challenges.

Like many new believers, I had countless questions. How does one cultivate a relationship with God? How do you hear His voice amidst the noise of everyday life? How do you distinguish His voice from your own thoughts? These were questions that echoed in my mind as I sought to deepen my understanding of God and His Word. I started to study the Bible diligently, praying for wisdom and insight. The King James Version became a source of spiritual nourishment, but I also explored other translations, such as the New International Version (NIV) and the Amplified Bible, to gain a broader understanding.

As I reflect on my journey, I cannot help but thank God for His unwavering presence in my life. Without Him, I would not be here, nor would my children. I mean that literally. God delivered my family and me from the hands of the enemy. The Apostle Paul reminds us in Ephesians 6:12, "For we wrestle not against flesh and blood, but against principalities, against powers, against the rulers of the darkness of this world, against spiritual wickedness in high places." This verse encapsulates what we experienced firsthand. We were unaware that the challenges we faced were not merely "bad days" but spiritual warfare manifesting in our lives.

It was not until we began to witness supernatural occurrences—demons and snakes appearing and disappearing—that I realized something was gravely wrong. What we thought were normal hardships were actual manifestations of spiritual forces working against us. This realization was a wake-up call, and it opened my eyes to the reality that many Christians are unaware of or unprepared for the spiritual battles we face.

The church I grew up in, like many others, did not teach us about spiritual warfare in a way that equipped us for the battles ahead. Perhaps our parents did encounter these realities but chose to shield us from them. Or maybe they did not know how to teach us from a biblical perspective. Whatever the case, I now understand that there are both physical and spiritual realms, and that the enemy can influence the physical through spiritual means.

Jealousy, envy, greed, pride, and pure wickedness can drive people to tap into dark spiritual forces, consciously or unconsciously. My story is a testimony to that truth. The purpose of writing this book is to awaken believers to the reality of spiritual warfare. The enemy will stop at nothing to prevent us from reaching our God-ordained purpose and destiny. We must be vigilant, prayerful, and armed with knowledge to fight this battle effectively.

As Christians, we all have a purpose for being here, and we are accountable for how we use our gifts and talents. When we stand before our Heaven Father, we will give an account of our lives. But we must also recognize that we have an adversary—the devil—who is constantly working against us. Unfortunately, many have perished spiritually because they did not know how to fight back. They did not understand what was happening to them, nor did they realize the spiritual dynamics at play.

For too many of us, our engagement with God's Word is sporadic at best. We pray occasionally, attend church regularly—or not—but we think that is enough. Yet, the enemy knows the vast potential God has placed within us, and he will do anything to stop us from walking in that potential.

Hosea 4:6 warns us, "My people are destroyed for lack of knowledge." It is my prayer that this book will be a source of knowledge and encouragement for you. Here is my story, and I hope it helps you recognize the seriousness of the spiritual battles we face and equips you to stand firm in your faith.

Chapter One

WHEN THE BATTLE HITS HOME—RECOGNIZING THE SPIRITUAL ATTACK

There is a moment in every believer's life when the battle becomes personal, when the enemy's attacks hit so close to home that you can no longer ignore them or chalk them up to mere coincidence. For me, that moment came after my father passed away. It seemed that from that point on, my life spiraled into chaos. Loss, fear, and confusion clouded my days, and the sense that I was under attack grew more palpable with each passing day.

The Bible tells us in 2 Corinthians 10:4, "For the weapons of our warfare are not carnal, but mighty through God to the pulling down of strongholds." At that time, I did not fully understand what it meant to engage in spiritual warfare. I had been raised in the church, but like many, I had not been taught to recognize the signs of spiritual attack or how to fight against it. But as the strange occurrences in my life began to escalate—seeing supernatural creatures, sensing evil presences in my home, and feeling the growing distance between myself and my children—I knew that something beyond the natural was at play.

It all started shortly after my father's death in January 2021. Just six months later, I had to give up my job, a role that I had dedicated myself to for years. I had recently purchased two cars—one for my son, who was on the verge of graduating college and heading to medical school, and one for myself. Yet, within weeks of buying the cars, I found myself unemployed, dealing with the aftermath of my father's death, and struggling to manage my family's affairs. Everything felt like it was falling apart.

The situation worsened when one evening, as I returned home from visiting my daughter, I encountered something so terrifying that I questioned my own sanity. I saw a creature unlike anything I had ever seen before—part human, part animal, with horns and a strange red glow. It was about four feet tall and stood in my driveway. My heart raced as I tried to comprehend what I was seeing. And then, just as quickly as it had appeared, it vanished. I was frozen in my car, terrified to step out, unsure of whether it would return. When I finally gathered the courage to go inside, my son stayed on the phone with me to ensure I made it in safely.

For days, I kept looking out for that creature, trying to process what I had seen. But I couldn't shake the fear or the sense that something was terribly wrong. My husband then shared his own strange experience—what he thought was a branch in the yard turned into a snake right before his eyes. It was clear that we were dealing with something far beyond the ordinary.

The Bible warns us in 1 Peter 5:8, "Be sober, be vigilant; because your adversary the devil, as a roaring lion, walketh about, seeking whom he may devour." This was no longer just a bad season—it was spiritual warfare. And yet, despite knowing that the enemy was attacking us, I did not know how to fight back. I did not know how to pray effectively or what to ask God for. I was desperate for answers but unsure of where to turn.

At night, my sleep became restless. I would feel the sensation of snakes slithering in my bed, waking up just before they could touch me. The fear was paralyzing, and I began to wonder if I was losing my mind. Who could I talk to about this? How could I explain what was happening without people thinking I was crazy? But deep down, I knew that this was not just my imagination. My husband had experienced it too, and that gave me some comfort. At least I was not alone.

Isaiah 54:17 became a lifeline for me during this time: "No weapon that is formed against thee shall prosper; and every tongue that shall rise against thee in judgment thou shalt condemn. This is the heritage of the servants of the Lord, and their righteousness is of me, saith the Lord." I clung to this promise, declaring it over my life, my marriage, and my children. I knew that the enemy had formed weapons against us, but I also knew that God's Word was true—those weapons would not prosper.

In my desperation, I reached out to a woman of God, someone I had prayed with before. When I told her what my husband and I had experienced, she confirmed what I feared: this was the work of the enemy. But she also reassured me that God's hand was protecting us. She prayed with me, and for a moment, I felt a sense of peace. But the battle was not over.

The attacks continued, and it became clear that they were not just aimed at me—they were targeting my children as well. My children were going through their own battles, experiencing nightmares and strange occurrences that they could not explain. But they kept it to themselves, afraid of how others might react if they spoke up. Communication between us began to break down, and tension filled our home. It was as if the enemy was trying to tear us apart from the inside out.

I could see in my children's eyes that something was not right, but I did not know how to help them. I prayed for them, but my prayers felt ineffective because I did not know what I was truly up against. It was not until later that I realized the enemy had been plotting to separate us—not just physically, but spiritually. The devil knew the calling on our lives, and he was doing everything in his power to prevent us from stepping into our God-given destinies.

But here is the truth that I want to share with you: No matter how fierce the battle, God is greater. The enemy may try to intimidate you with fear, confusion, and chaos, but he cannot defeat you if you are rooted in Christ. The weapons of our warfare are mighty through God. We may not always know what we are fighting against, but God does, and He has already given us the victory through Jesus Christ.

Psalm 91:11-12 gives us this promise: "For He shall give His angels charge over thee, to keep thee in all thy ways. They shall bear thee up in their hands, lest thou dash thy foot against a stone." God is our protector, our refuge, and our strength. When the enemy comes against us like a flood, God raises a standard against him (Isaiah 59:19). No matter what the enemy tries to throw at you—whether it is fear, loss, or division—God's hand is upon you, and His protection is over you.

I encourage you today, if you are facing a battle that seems insurmountable, know that God is with you. He has equipped you with His Word, His Spirit, and His promises. Stand firm in your faith, and do not be shaken by the attacks of the enemy. As Paul reminds us in Ephesians 6:13, "Wherefore take unto you the whole armor of God, that ye may be able to withstand in the evil day, and having done all, to stand." You are not fighting alone. God is fighting for you, and He will bring you through victorious.

This chapter of my life was difficult, but it taught me that the spiritual realm is real, and the enemy is relentless in his pursuit to derail God's plans for us. But it also taught me that God's power is greater, and His promises are unshakable. I pray that as you read this book, you will be encouraged to trust in God's protection, stand firm in your faith, and recognize the spiritual battles for what they are—temporary challenges that will ultimately lead to victory in Christ.

Chapter Two

THE ENEMY'S SUBTLE ATTACK—GUARDING WHAT GOD HAS BLESSED

Raising children in today's world is no easy task. There are countless temptations and distractions that can easily lead young hearts astray. But by God's grace, my children were raised in a God-fearing home. From the moment they could speak, I taught them how to pray and shared the Word of God with them. My husband and I didn't just teach the Bible; we lived it. We modeled a life of faith, obedience, and devotion to God.

Our home was filled with love and the presence of God. We enjoyed being together, and our family thrived on the foundation of prayer and the Word. As they grew older and went off to college, my children would call me every day. We would talk about life, but most importantly, we would talk about the Lord. Their relationship with God continued to flourish even as they stepped into the world on their own.

People often admired my children and would ask me, "How were you able to raise them in this world, with everything going on? With all the temptations of drugs and alcohol, how did you keep them grounded?" My answer was always the same: "It is God." I never took the credit for their lives. I knew it was God's hand guiding and protecting them. But little did I know, the enemy was watching too. The devil was not happy with the peace, love, and blessings in our home, and envy was beginning to rise.

The Bible warns us in 1 Peter 5:8, "Be sober, be vigilant; because your adversary the devil, as a roaring lion, walketh about, seeking whom he may devour." As I reflect on those days, I realize now that the enemy was seeking an entry point into our lives. He saw how God had blessed us, and in his jealousy, he began to look for ways to disrupt our peace and attack what God had built.

At first, it seemed like normal growing pains—my children were becoming more independent, making their own decisions, and learning about life on their own terms. People around me would say, "Oh, they're just adulting. They're figuring out who they are." But in my spirit, I knew it was more than that. I could sense that something was not right. The enemy had turned my children against me, and his goal was to disgrace them and take their lives. The unity and peace that once filled our home were being eroded, and I knew I had a problem.

When things began to spiral out of control, I reached out to the woman of God who had prayed with me before. She was a spiritual warrior, someone who understood the power of prayer and fasting. I told her what was happening, and she immediately discerned that this was a spiritual attack. She instructed me to fast for three days—from six in the morning until six in the evening—and to pray fervently for my family.

Fasting is a powerful weapon in spiritual warfare. It humbles us before God and brings clarity and strength in the midst of the battle. Isaiah 58:6 says, "Is not this the fast that I have chosen? to loose the bands of wickedness, to undo the heavy burdens, and to let the oppressed go free, and that ye break every yoke?" I knew that I needed God to break the yokes that the enemy had placed on my family. So I fasted and prayed, trusting that God would intervene.

Chapter Three

DIVINE INTERVENTION— WHEN GOD REVEALS THE ENEMY'S PLANS

A few days after my fast, my sister Kate, who lives in Africa, called me. She shared that she had spoken with her pastor about me, asking him to pray for my situation. A few days later, the pastor called her back with a message. He told her to tell me that in three months, God was going to shock me with a miracle, but that I needed to pray for seven days in preparation.

I was determined to follow through with the pastor's instruction, but every time I started the seven days of prayer, something would happen to stop me. Either I would fall ill, something would happen with my children or husband, or some other distraction would arise. The enemy was working overtime to prevent me from completing the prayer, and this cycle of interruptions continued for the entire three months. Even the woman of God called me one day and said that the Lord wanted me to pray for seven days. But no matter how hard I tried, something always got in the way.

As the end of the three-month period approached, I was beginning to lose hope. But then, on December 3, 2021, something remarkable happened. Kate called me again, excitedly sharing that a pastor she and her husband had recently met was coming to their home to pray with them. They didn't know this pastor well, but God had used him to speak a powerful word to her husband, so they invited him to their home for prayer.

While the pastor was there, Kate asked him if he would say a word of prayer for me, specifically asking God to bless me with a job. The pastor agreed, but instead of just offering a quick prayer, he asked to speak with me directly. When Kate handed him the phone, I wasn't expecting much. I thought he would simply pray for a job as requested. But as he began to pray, he started revealing things about my life that I had never shared with anyone.

He described the spiritual attacks I had been facing, the plans the enemy had set in motion against me, and the struggles my family had been enduring. He spoke with such accuracy that it overwhelmed me. I knew that this was a divine encounter. The pastor was speaking directly from the Spirit of God, revealing the enemy's schemes and confirming what I had sensed in my spirit all along.

Romans 8:31 reassures us, "If God be for us, who can be against us?" In that moment, I felt the truth of this scripture in a powerful way. No matter how hard the enemy tried to destroy me and my family, God was with us. He was fighting on our behalf, revealing the enemy's plans, and providing the strength and guidance we needed to overcome.

The pastor told me that God was not done with me and that this was just the beginning of the battle. He encouraged me to stay strong, to keep praying, and to trust that God would bring us through. After the call ended, Kate was just as overwhelmed as I was. She kept repeating, "I didn't tell him anything," and I knew she had not. Some of the things the pastor revealed were things even she did not know. It was clear that God was orchestrating this entire encounter.

From that day on, everything about my life began to unfold. God started revealing the spiritual forces at work and showing me how to fight back. But it was not an overnight fix. The road to victory required persistence, faith, and a willingness to let God do the work in me. I had made a mess of things in many areas of my life, but God was faithful. He was showing me that even In the midst of chaos and spiritual attack, He was still in control.

THE UNSEEN WAR: MY ENCOUNTER WITH FAITH AND DARKNESS

I learned that the enemy's plans are no match for God's purpose. The devil may plot and scheme, but God is always several steps ahead. He knows how to turn the enemy's attacks into opportunities for growth and deliverance. As Romans 8:28 reminds us, "And we know that all things work together for good to them that love God, to them who are the called according to his purpose."

This experience taught me that spiritual warfare is real, but so is God's power. When we stay close to Him, seek His guidance, and trust in His promises, no weapon formed against us can prosper. The battle may be fierce, but victory is certain because God is on our side. He is our protector, our deliverer, and the One who fights for us when we are too weak to fight for ourselves.

As you read this chapter, I pray that you are encouraged to stand firm in your faith. No matter what the enemy throws at you, remember that God is greater. He has already won the victory, and He will carry you through every trial, every storm, and every spiritual battle. Keep praying, keep trusting, and know that God is working on your behalf. You are not alone in this fight—God is with you, and He will never leave you nor forsake you.

Chapter Four

THE POWER OF FASTING
AND DELIVERANCE

The next morning, Pastor Ben called me. His voice was steady, carrying a weight that told me he had something important to share. "The Lord wants you to fast and pray for three days," he said. He didn't leave it at that. He sent me specific scriptures from the book of Psalms, and I was to read and meditate on them during this time of fasting.

I had fasted before, but this time felt different. There was an urgency, a divine assignment that I could not quite grasp yet. On the first night of the fast, as the hunger pangs gnawed at my stomach, I found solace in the Word. As I read and prayed, a sense of peace settled over me, but it was soon interrupted by a phone call from Pastor Ben.

"God has revealed one of your enemies to me," he said. His words were chilling, yet I felt a strange sense of confirmation. Deep down, I knew that this fast was stirring things in the spiritual realm, uncovering secrets that had been hidden for far too long.

The second night, something unsettling happened. My husband, usually calm and composed, walked into our room, his face pale and his hands trembling. "Something happened to me last night," he confessed. His voice was shaky, filled with a fear I had never seen in him before. "I thought I was going to die, but I can't explain what I felt."

I did not know what to say. How could I comfort him when I did not understand what was happening myself? "I'm sorry you had a bad night," I said gently, "Maybe tomorrow will be better." But even as I spoke those words, I could not shake the feeling that something much deeper was going on.

On the third day of the fast, I woke up early, determined to finish the scriptures and prayer. But as I read the last verse, something strange began to happen. My body started to shake uncontrollably. Nausea swept over me, and I struggled to keep reading. "If I could just finish this last scripture," I kept telling myself, trying to push through the discomfort.

But the shaking intensified. I fell to my knees, clutching the Bible in my lap. My hands became paralyzed, and all I could manage to say was, "Thank you, Jesus." Over and over, I whispered those words, clinging to them like a lifeline. My eyes were closed, but when I finally opened them, I saw it—a ray of light, like something was leaving my body.

It felt as though a heavy weight had been lifted off me. My hands slowly regained feeling, and after a few minutes, I was able to get off the floor. My stomach felt like it had broken loose, and I was left weak, but with a strange sense of relief.

My husband, concerned by the sight of me on the floor, asked what had happened. I described the experience to him, and he listened intently. "That was the same way I felt yesterday," he said, his voice filled with awe and confusion.

I was too weak to make sense of it all, but I knew something significant had occurred. I called Pastor Ben and Kate to share what had happened, and they both confirmed it—"You were delivered," they said.

"Delivered from what?" I asked, still reeling from the experience. They explained that something had been put on me, something dark and oppressive, but it was gone now. I was confused and overwhelmed. "Who, why, and when?" I wondered aloud, struggling to piece together the puzzle of this spiritual battle.

Chapter Five

UNMASKING THE ENEMY WITHIN

As I reflected on the events of those three days, one thought kept gnawing at me—our enemies are often closer than we think. The ones who know us best, who claim to love us the most, are sometimes the very ones the devil uses to attack us. I couldn't help but think of the story of Cain and Abel. Jealousy and envy drove Cain to murder his own brother, and that same spirit seemed to be at work in my life.

Just when I thought the battle was over, Pastor Ben called again. "The Lord wants us to pray for seven days," he said. I sighed inwardly. Seven days of prayer and fasting. It seemed like every time I turned around, the number seven was coming up again. But I knew better than to ignore a divine directive, so I agreed.

The first day of the fast passed uneventfully, but on the second day, Pastor Ben was almost in a car accident. The enemy was already at work, trying to disrupt our prayers. On the third day, his wife's shop was attacked by rats—they came in and ate all her goods, destroying everything. On the fourth day, some unknown persons approached Pastor Ben, telling him to stop praying for me. "Things are getting out of hand," they warned him.

By the fifth day, the attacks were relentless. My husband was growing increasingly worried about me. "Maybe you should take a break from praying so much," he suggested, concern etched on his face. I wasn't feeling well either, but I knew I couldn't stop now. We were in the midst of a spiritual war, and giving up wasn't an option.

On the sixth day, Pastor Ben's eye started swelling for no apparent reason. And then, as if things couldn't get worse, he almost died at a gas station. A fire broke out, trapping him in his car with no way to escape. It was a miracle that he made it out alive.

I don't even remember what happened on the seventh day, but I do know that those seven days were some of the most intense and terrifying days of my life. Death and destruction seemed to be all around me. We were praying for five hours a day, pushing through exhaustion and fear. I had never prayed like that before, but I knew that our only hope was in God.

After those seven days, we kept praying—another seven days, and another, until it turned into months of unceasing prayer. Every day, we battled in the spiritual realm, seeking God's deliverance and protection. And during that time, God began to show me things, revealing the truth about my enemies and the darkness that had been surrounding me.

I couldn't believe it at first. The people I thought were my friends, the ones I loved and trusted—they were the very ones who had been used against me. It was shocking, just as the Lord had said it would be. But in His mercy, God didn't show me everything all at once. He revealed the truth gradually, allowing me to process and heal from the betrayal.

Through it all, I learned that even in the darkest of times, God is with us. He protects us, guides us, and delivers us from the enemy's grasp. The battle is real, but so is the victory. And as I continued to pray and seek God, I found hope and strength in His unwavering love.

Chapter Six

THE MASK UNVEILED

I always thought of her as my sister, even though technically she was my half-sister. To me, the fact that we had different mothers did not matter. We shared the same father, and that was enough. Our relationship did not blossom overnight; it took time. I met her when I was 18, but we did not really start connecting until a few years before my father passed away. Then, one day out of the blue, she called me.

She said she had been at church, and her pastor told the congregation to find someone they trusted to pray with and share their personal struggles. She told me my name kept coming up in her spirit, so she decided to call. I was surprised, but I saw it as an opportunity to finally have the kind of sisterly bond I had always wanted. How naïve I was.

The entire time, she was gathering information from me, using it in ways I could never have imagined. I used to confide in her about the bad dreams I had been having, and she would just listen, never saying much. Little did I know, I was feeding the enemy every time I opened my mouth.

In hindsight, I can see that I was not completely comfortable sharing everything with her, and I am grateful for that now. I told her enough to harm me, but not everything. I could never have guessed that the person I was confiding in was the one plotting against me. We developed a relationship of sorts—one that I thought was rooted in trust and prayer. We prayed together every Friday, talking about our lives. But she would say strange things about my father, things that did not make sense. I chose to ignore them because I was not interested in his properties like she was.

It was not until after my father died that I discovered the truth. She was not even his biological daughter, and he knew it before he died. I was stunned. A day before his death, she called me, asking if I would go with her to Africa to convince him to give her power of attorney over his properties. I was shocked. Why did she think she needed that? Weren't they close enough for him to have already done so? She did not have a good answer, and I decided to stay out of it.

Another time, she called to say my father had insulted her, calling her a liar, a thief, and a wicked person. Those words were so unlike him that I did not know what to think. When I asked her why he would say such things, she claimed he was getting old and wanted to go back to Africa to see a girlfriend he had not seen in years. It did not add up. So, I called my father, who told me he was going home to divide his properties to avoid confusion after his death. I did not ask about the insults she claimed he threw at her. I just pleaded with him not to go, but he never came back to the States.

Years passed, and our relationship grew, but something was always off. She seemed to be more interested in my father's properties than in building a relationship with me or with him. Yet, I was so caught up in finally having a sister that I ignored all the warning signs.

Looking back, I see how innocent I was, how blind to the reality of the situation. My gut had tried to warn me, but I brushed it off. After all, she was my sister—what harm could she do? But harm she did. Hate, envy, and jealousy had been brewing all along, and I was oblivious, walking in a fantasy world of what I thought sisterhood should be.

When dealing with relationships, especially within families, it is crucial to seek God's wisdom. Proverbs 3:5-6 reminds us to "Trust in the Lord with all thine heart and lean not unto thine own understanding; in all your ways acknowledge Him, and

He shall direct your paths." Sometimes, our feelings of unease are the Holy Spirit's way of guiding us. Psalm 55:12-14 reflects the pain of betrayal by someone close: "For it is not an enemy who reproaches me; then I could have borne it. But it was you, a man my equal, my companion and my acquaintance." Even when betrayal comes, God offers healing and wisdom to move forward.

Chapter Seven
THE SUBTLE REJECTION

I remember the day my oldest son graduated from high school. My half-sister and I weren't particularly close at that time, but she came to the graduation as a representative for my father, who was in Africa. After the ceremony and the party that followed, I walked her to her car, thanking her for coming. As we walked, I held her hand, sharing how well things were going, how wonderful my husband had been, and how much he had helped me put together the party.

Then, without warning, she jerked her hand away from mine. It was such a small, quick gesture, but it felt like a slap in the face. I was confused, wondering what had caused her to react that way. But, as always, I dismissed it, telling myself it was not a big deal.

Now, looking back, I realize that moment was a reflection of the deeper issues in our relationship. It was not just a random act; it was a glimpse into the envy and jealousy that had been simmering beneath the surface. But at the time, I just let it go, never imagining the depth of the betrayal that was to come.

Sometimes, the smallest actions can reveal the true nature of a person's heart. It is important to be discerning and to listen to the Holy Spirit's promptings. Proverbs 4:23 advises us to "Keep thy heart with all diligence, for out of it are the issues of life." If something feels off, do not be quick to dismiss it. Seek God's wisdom in prayer, and He will reveal the truth in His time. Galatians 6:9 encourages us, "And let us not be weary in well doing, for in due season we shall reap, if we faint not." Keep your trust in God, and He will guide you through even the most challenging relationships.

Chapter Eight

THE RING AND THE UNSEEN STRUGGLE

When I married my husband, my father was living in the United States, but he could not attend our wedding due to a hip replacement surgery. After the wedding, my husband and our children visited him. During our visit, I showed my father the ring my husband had given me. Unexpectedly, someone close to us grabbed my hand and began twisting my finger roughly to inspect the ring, as if she wanted to wrench it from my hand. The pain caught me off guard, and I wondered what was happening, but I chose to remain silent.

Over the years, whenever my father planned a visit to the USA, she would be the one to call and inform me. I often wondered why she would do this when my father could easily call me himself. The only time I would hear from her was when my father was about to visit, and I found this behavior strange, though I dismissed it, thinking perhaps she was just trying to be nice.

It was not until much later that I realized she had a hidden motive. Her calls were part of a strategy to paint a favorable picture of herself to my father. Once he was under this influence, he would talk to me and share updates about my family. After our conversation, he would report back to her, unknowingly providing her with information about our lives, our children's progress, and our plans for the future.

What I did not know was that she would take this information and use it against us, working behind the scenes to ensure that our plans would fail. For years, my family faced unexplained setbacks. Our children's educational achievements, career opportunities, and even our basic needs like housing and food became constant struggles. We were baffled by the relentless difficulties and could not understand why things were not working out.

In hindsight, I realized that we often dismissed these challenges as mere life circumstances—bad days or just the natural ebb and flow of life. But deep down, I knew something more sinister was at play, even though I could not quite put my finger on it.

The Bible says in Ephesians 6:12: "For we wrestle not against flesh and blood, but against principalities, against powers, against the rulers of the darkness of this world, against spiritual wickedness in high places." This verse came to life as I began to understand that our struggles were not just physical but deeply spiritual. I learned that we must be vigilant and prayerful, discerning the schemes of the enemy who often works through people close to us to bring about our downfall.

Chapter Nine

THE LIGHT SHINES IN THE DARKNESS

One particular incident stands out in my memory. My husband, despite being a college graduate, went out one day to apply for a job delivering bread—a job far below his qualifications—only to be turned down. Everywhere we turned, doors seemed to slam shut in our faces. We faced rejection after rejection, and it felt like an invisible force was working against us.

Yet, through all of this, I was aware of God's presence. Even when everything around us was falling apart, I had a deep sense that God was with us, guiding and protecting us. The situations we faced might have seemed ordinary on the surface, but they carried a deeper spiritual significance.

It was not until later, when God began to reveal the truth, that I started piecing together the puzzle. The subtle manipulations and the spiritual warfare we were unknowingly engaged in became clear. The Bible warns us in 1 Peter 5:8: "Be sober, be vigilant; because your adversary the devil, as a roaring lion, walketh about, seeking whom he may devour." This scripture reminds us that the devil is always on the prowl, looking for ways to destroy us. He operates in the shadows, using deceit and cunning to achieve his aims.

For years, I had dismissed the spiritual aspect of our struggles. But now, I understood that the devil is not only a thief but also a master deceiver. He often works through those who are closest to us, using them as instruments of his wicked plans. This realization led me to the importance of putting on the whole armor of God, as described in Ephesians 6:11-18: "Put on the whole armor of God, that ye may be able to stand against the wiles of the devil."

We are instructed to equip ourselves with the belt of truth, the breastplate of righteousness, the shield of faith, the helmet of salvation, and the sword of the Spirit, which is the word of God. These spiritual tools are essential for standing firm against the attacks of the enemy. I learned that prayer is our most potent weapon, and through it, we can break the chains of the enemy's stronghold over our lives.

Looking back, I can see how God was protecting and preserving us, even in the darkest times. The enemy might have had his plans, but God's purpose for our lives was far greater. He allowed us to go through these trials to strengthen our faith, build our character, and draw us closer to Him.

Romans 8:28 says, "And we know that all things work together for good to them that love God, to them who are called according to his purpose." This verse became a source of comfort and hope for me, reminding me that no matter what we go through, God is working it all out for our good.

Chapter Ten

HIDDEN AGENDAS

Beneath the Surface: Finding Hope and Healing in the Shadows

For 34 years, there was an absence of real connection between Lamia and me. Our lives seemed to drift in separate currents, making any bond between us elusive. Living in different states only reinforced this separation. The rare occasions when my father visited America were the only times Lamia would reach out. However, her motives were not to build a relationship but rather to monitor how much I knew and what information my father shared about me.

One vivid memory stands out from those years. When my oldest son was born, we lived in an apartment complex divided into four separate units. Lamia resided in the unit downstairs, while my first husband and I lived directly above her. My father was also on the top floor, next to us. Despite our close physical proximity, Lamia never once visited me or offered to see the newborn. Her absence during such a pivotal moment in my life was striking. It seemed she had no interest in our daily lives or in forming any familial bond.

However, the dynamics shifted when marital issues arose between my ex-husband and me. Lamia suddenly became involved, offering advice and reassurances. Her concern, though well-meaning, felt insincere because it came at a time of crisis rather than through genuine interest or support. She seldom came upstairs to visit or engage in meaningful conversation. Instead, her interactions with me were limited to brief encounters outside or on rare occasions when I ventured downstairs to meet her and her boyfriend.

One particularly tumultuous day, feeling utterly overwhelmed by the problems in my marriage, I ran out of the house and down the road, seeking some form of relief or escape from the turmoil. To my astonishment, Lamia appeared and tried to console me. Her sudden show of empathy was confusing, as I had never felt a real connection with her before. It was as if her concern was a façade, appearing only when it was convenient for her.

This experience revealed a troubling reality: people often project a veneer of spirituality or concern without true substance. They might invoke God's name, yet their actions and intentions can be far from genuine. This dissonance can lead to misleading expectations and confusion, especially when we hope for change or support from those who seem spiritually aligned.

The Bible offers profound insights into the themes of deliverance and healing, reinforcing the hope that God can bring about true transformation and support even in the most challenging circumstances. In Isaiah 61:1, it is written: "The Spirit of the Lord GOD is on me, because the LORD has anointed me to preach good tidings unto the meek; He hath sent me to bind up the brokenhearted, to proclaim liberty to the captives, and the opening of the prison to them that are bound." This verse highlights God's promise of deliverance and healing for those who are suffering and in need of restoration.

Another powerful scripture is found in Psalm 34:17-18: "The righteous cry, and the LORD heareth, and deliver them out of all their troubles. The LORD is close to the brokenhearted and saves those who are crushed in spirit." This passage reassures us that even when we feel isolated or misunderstood, God is near and ready to provide deliverance from our troubles and comfort those who are hurting.

The New Testament also emphasizes the transformative power of Christ's deliverance. In Luke 4:18, Jesus declares: "The Spirit of the Lord is on me, because he has anointed me to preach the gospel to the poor; He has sent me to heal the brokenhearted, to preach deliverance to the captives, and recovery of sight to the blind, to set at liberty them that are bruised." This promise reflects Jesus' mission to bring liberation and healing to those in bondage, both physically and spiritually.

Reflecting on these scriptures, it becomes evident that true deliverance comes from a divine source and not merely from human gestures or superficial connections. While Lamia's actions revealed a lack of genuine care, the hope we find in God's promises provides a more profound and lasting comfort. The assurance of God's presence and His commitment to deliver and heal us from all forms of bondage and distress offers a beacon of hope and a reminder that our ultimate source of support and transformation comes from Him.

In these moments of disillusionment and confusion, it is essential to remember that while human relationships may fall short, God's promises remain steadfast. Through Him, we find true deliverance, healing, and hope, reinforcing the belief that our struggles are not in vain but are met with divine support and eventual restoration.

Chapter Eleven

UNVEILING HIDDEN MOTIVES

Beneath the Surface: Finding Hope and Healing in the Shadows

A lot was happening in my life as I began to know my father better, and perhaps there was a bit of jealousy involved. Daddy started paying more attention to me than to the rest of my siblings. His relationship with Lamia was particularly strained due to her lifestyle choices, which he disapproved of. I understood the tension and decided to let it go, not wanting to exacerbate the situation. So, when Lamia called after 34 years, talking about her pastor and finding someone she could trust, I was genuinely happy. I thought it might be a fresh start for both of us, an opportunity to connect as adults and finally build the relationship I had always hoped for.

We were young at the time, and I thought that this new chapter in our lives might bring us closer. I had remarried, and Lamia had also married, so I figured our lives had changed enough to allow for a new beginning. I approached the situation with optimism, believing that we could finally appreciate one another and develop a meaningful relationship. Life had indeed changed for both of us, and I hoped this would be a turning point.

Looking back, about a year before my father passed away, I received a friend request on Facebook from someone named Kate, who claimed to be another daughter of my father. I couldn't remember her at the time, so I called Lamia, who had become my praying partner. When I asked Lamia if she knew who Kate was, she quickly dismissed her, saying, "Is she the one in a red outfit on Facebook? I don't know her. Don't befriend her!" Trusting Lamia, I followed her advice and didn't pursue the connection further.

A few months later, Kate reached out again, introducing herself as Daddy's daughter. This time, I called Lamia and asked her again if she knew Kate. Her response was puzzling: "Oh, yes, I remember now. It's all coming back to me." I was confused, as she had previously denied knowing her. When I reminded her of this, she simply said, "Oh yes, I didn't remember at the time." Once again, I let it go, not wanting to create any tension.

As I began talking more with Kate, we had lovely conversations, sharing stories and learning about each other. I told Kate about my wonderful relationship with Lamia, how we prayed together and studied the Bible, and how I wished she could get to know Lamia too. Encouraged, Kate reached out to Lamia, but her attempts were met with a cold response. When I asked Lamia why she hadn't responded to Kate, she made excuses about being too busy but promised to make an effort. Unfortunately, that effort never materialized.

Despite Lamia's indifference, I continued building my relationship with Kate. A few months before Daddy passed away, Kate expressed a deep desire to visit him. She lived in another country and hadn't seen Daddy for over 30 years. I encouraged her, saying it was a good idea. Lamia had earlier mentioned wanting to visit Daddy in January 2021, but it wasn't feasible for me at the time. I didn't mention Kate's plans to Lamia because of her lack of interest in Kate and because I felt that if Kate wanted to reconnect with Daddy, it should be their personal decision. I didn't want to meddle in their relationship, just as I hadn't interfered in Lamia's relationship with Daddy.

Around the same time, Lamia visited me, marking only the second time she had ever come to my home. Her first visit had been years earlier, during my daughter's high school graduation, and she had brought Daddy along. This time, she came with her husband and one of our cousins on my father's side. Although I knew the cousin, we weren't particularly close. They were only staying for one day, but I noticed that Lamia had brought an unusually large suitcase. I thought it was odd, but I didn't comment. During their stay, we attended a funeral together, and I met more of my extended family. Despite the brief visit, I enjoyed reconnecting with my relatives.

After they left, I began reflecting on the peculiarities of Lamia's behavior. I recalled how, during one of my visits to her, I had noticed that a pair of shoes I loved had gone missing. The shoes were a unique color, and I had received many compliments on them, so I remembered them well. When I got home and discovered they weren't in my luggage, I asked Lamia if I had left them at her place. She said no, and I let it go, though the incident stuck with me.

I also remembered the time she gave me a bag of clothes from Africa, supposedly from her cousin on her mom's side, claiming they didn't fit her. As I tried them on, she lay on the bed, watching me closely. It struck me that she might have done something to those clothes, but I didn't want to believe it. Similarly, when she visited me with that oversized suitcase, I later discovered that my camera bag, a cherished gift from my mom when I was 20, had gone missing. Lamia knew about the camera, and although I didn't realize it was gone until much later, I eventually connected the dots.

These incidents began to reveal a troubling pattern in our relationship. What I had initially hoped would be a new beginning, a chance to build a genuine bond, was clouded by deception and hidden motives. The Bible warns us about trusting too easily without discernment. In Matthew 7:15-16, Jesus cautions, "Beware of false prophets, which come to you in sheep's clothing, but inwardly are ravenous wolves. Ye shall know them by their fruits." This passage reminds us to be vigilant and discerning in our relationships, even with those who appear to be close to us.

Through these experiences, I learned that not all relationships are as they seem on the surface. But even in the midst of betrayal and disappointment, God offers hope and deliverance. Psalm 34:17-18 reassures us: "The righteous cry, and the LORD heareth, and deliver them out of all their troubles. The LORD is close to the brokenhearted and saves those who are crushed in spirit." Despite the challenges, I found solace in knowing that God is always near, ready to deliver us from our troubles and heal our broken hearts.

Chapter Twelve
THE PRICE OF TRUST

Meeting my father at 18 was a significant moment in my life, and it was also when I first met Lamia as an adult. My father gave me a unique necklace that held a special place in my heart. It was designed to spin around, revealing the words "I love you." At the time, I didn't realize that Lamia might have been envious of this gift. However, as our relationship evolved into a closer bond, I began to notice unsettling signs.

During our time as prayer partners, I was surprised to see Lamia wearing an identical necklace. I couldn't help but think that she had deliberately duplicated the one Daddy had given me. It struck me as strange, but I chose not to say anything. I wanted to believe that our relationship was sincere and that these little things didn't matter. Yet, deep down, I could not shake the feeling that something was off.

About a year into our prayer partnership, Lamia asked me about the necklace Daddy had given me. I explained that it had been stolen, expecting some sort of reaction from her. Instead, she remained silent, offering no sympathy or concern. Her lack of response was odd, but I brushed it off, not wanting to create any tension. I had grown up without a sister, and my cousins on my mom's side got along relatively well. The small things that bothered me about Lamia seemed insignificant in comparison to the joy I felt in finally having a sister. I did not want to jeopardize our relationship over what I thought were trivial matters.

But as time went on, these small incidents began to add up. I could not ignore the nagging feeling that something was wrong. The Bible teaches us that the Holy Spirit often speaks to us through our conscience, warning us of danger or deceit. Proverbs 3:5-6 advises, "Trust in the LORD with all thine heart; and lean not unto tine own understanding; in all thy ways acknowledge him, and he shall direct thy paths." I realized that my desire to maintain a relationship with Lamia had clouded my judgment. I had ignored the subtle warnings that God had placed in my heart.

God's Spirit never leaves us; it is we who sometimes drift away from Him. In John 16:13, Jesus promises, "Howbeit when He, the Spirit of truth, is come, he will guide you into all truth." This assurance reminded me that God is always ready to guide us back to the right path, even when we have been led astray by our own desires or by the deception of others.

As I reflected on my relationship with Lamia, I began to see the signs I had missed earlier. The stolen necklace, the missing shoes, the camera bag—all these were not just coincidences. They were warnings that I had ignored in my eagerness to maintain a bond with my sister. But God, in His infinite wisdom, was revealing the truth to me in His own time.

This realization was painful, but it also brought a sense of clarity and peace. I understood that while human relationships can be flawed and deceptive, God's love and guidance are perfect and unchanging. The Bible reassures us in Psalm 32:7, "Thou art my hiding place; Thou shalt preserve me from trouble; Thou shalt compass me about with songs of deliverance." This verse became a source of comfort as I navigated the complexities of my relationship with Lamia.

Chapter Thirteen

THE DECEPTIVE FACADE

Beneath the Surface: A Journey of Faith and Family

Lamia always presented herself as sweet and gentle, a woman with a quiet demeanor that endeared her to many. To the outside world, she appeared loving and caring, a person who could do no wrong. My family, along with many others, were completely taken in by her facade. However, as time went on, I began to realize that things were not as they seemed. My father, who had a deep understanding of human nature, was not fooled. He often warned us about Lamia, describing her as wicked. My sister Lily, who took care of my father in Africa, would often rebuke him for saying such things, insisting that he was wrong. But my father, with a grave tone, would say, "Wait until I die, and you will see the wickedness of your so-called Sister Lamia. All hell is going to break loose." His words echoed in my mind, but I dismissed them, thinking it was the paranoia of an old man. Unfortunately, his prediction came true, and after his death, the turmoil began.

When my husband first met Lamia, he confided in me that he felt an inexplicable strife whenever she was around. I couldn't understand why he felt that way. After all, she was my sister, and I loved her. I believed that all she wanted from me was love, and I wanted nothing more than to be close to her. However, my husband's intuition troubled me. He reminded me of an incident during our wedding preparations when Lamia had asked me to pay her way to attend because she was broke. My husband had found it odd and unsettling. Then, after our wedding, she called me asking for $5,000 to stop her house from going into foreclosure. I was taken aback by her request. We had just gotten married, and I couldn't ask my husband for such a large sum, especially since he barely knew her. At that time, Lamia and I were not as close as we would later become through prayer, so I declined her request, which left me feeling uneasy.

As the years passed, I couldn't shake off the feeling that something was off. My father's words haunted me, and my husband's warnings rang true. Lamia's actions, though subtle, started to reveal her true nature. She would say things that contradicted her earlier statements, and I began to notice a pattern of manipulation and deceit. My father had seen through her, and now I was starting to see it too.

The Bible warns us in 2 Corinthians 11:14-15, "And no marvel; for Satan himself is transformed into an angel of light". It is not surprising, then, if his servants also masquerade as servants of righteousness. Their end will be what their actions deserve." Lamia's behavior reminded me of this verse, as she had fooled many with her angelic facade, yet underneath it lay a heart filled with wickedness and deception. The spiritual strife my husband sensed was not unfounded; it was a manifestation of the spiritual battle raging beneath the surface.

As I began to pray more earnestly, seeking God's wisdom and discernment, I realized that I needed to protect my family from the toxic influence that Lamia was bringing into our lives. Ephesians 6:12 reminds us, "For we wrestle not against flesh and blood, but against principalities, against powers, against the rulers of the darkness of this world, against spiritual wickedness in high places." This scripture gave me the strength to stand firm in the spiritual warfare that had subtly invaded my family.

I prayed for deliverance, not just for myself, but for my entire family. I asked God to reveal the truth and to protect us from the enemy's schemes. As I continued to seek God's guidance, He began to unveil the reality of the situation. The once hidden motives and actions of Lamia started to become clear, and I saw the need to distance myself from her influence.

Psalm 91:3-4 provided me with the assurance I needed: "Surely He shall deliver thee from the snare of the fowler and from the noisome pestilence. He shall cover thee with his feathers, and under his wings shalt thou trust: His truth shall be thy shield and buckler." I held onto this promise, knowing that God would protect us from the snares set by the enemy.

The journey was not easy, but through prayer and the Word of God, I found the strength to confront the reality of Lamia's deception. I had to make difficult decisions, but I did so with the confidence that God was with me. He delivered me from the strife that Lamia brought into our lives and gave me the peace that surpasses all understanding.

As I look back, I am grateful for the discernment that God provided. My father's warnings, my husband's intuition, and the Scriptures all aligned to reveal the truth. God's Word is a lamp to our feet and a light to our path (Psalm 119:105), guiding us through the darkness and leading us to safety. In the end, it was God's deliverance that saved us from the turmoil that threatened to engulf our family. I found peace in knowing that no weapon formed against us would prosper (Isaiah 54:17), and that God's protection and deliverance are always assured for those who trust in Him.

Chapter Fourteen

UNMASKING THE PAST

When the Ebola outbreak struck Africa, Lamia, her husband, and their adopted daughter were forced to return to the United States. I still remember the day she called me from the airport, stranded and desperate for help. They were stuck at JFK Airport without the fare to get to their destination, and she asked me to buy their tickets. Although surprised that she turned to me for help, I was also touched. Our relationship was not particularly close at the time, but I was happy to help. It brought back memories of the time I spent with her and my father when I first met them.

I had met my father for the first time at the age of 18, and during that time, I stayed with him and Lamia's older sister, Rossie. Those were formative years for me, and I was eager to build relationships with my newfound family. But as I grew closer to them, I began to notice things that troubled me. Rossie, for instance, began making advances towards me that were inappropriate and confusing. Homosexuality was not openly discussed in those days, and I was completely unprepared to handle the situation. My father was oblivious to what was happening, and I was left feeling isolated and unsure of whom to trust.

Eventually, the situation became unbearable, and I moved out of my father's house to stay with Lamia. But even there, I couldn't escape the past. Rossie showed up at Lamia's

- 34 -

house, uninvited, and continued her inappropriate behavior. I felt trapped and alone, unable to share my experiences with anyone. Lamia, instead of supporting me, seemed to distance herself from the situation. She told her friends that Rossie wasn't gay until I came to live with them, insinuating that I had somehow caused her sister's behavior. This betrayal hurt deeply, and I realized that my relationship with Lamia would never be what I had hoped.

Years later, after my father had passed away and Lamia and I had reconnected through our prayer partnership, she revealed to me that Rossie had come out of the closet and was no longer hiding her sexuality. Lamia suggested that we reach out to Rossie and try to build a relationship with her, claiming that she had changed and was no longer living that lifestyle. I hesitated, unsure of whether Rossie had truly changed, but I agreed to reach out to her. After talking with her, I didn't get the sense that she had genuinely turned her life around, and I told Lamia that we should keep her in our prayers.

The entire situation was a painful reminder of the challenges I had faced in my early years with my father's children. It seemed that no matter how much time had passed, the wounds from those years had never fully healed. Lamia's behavior continued to raise questions in my mind. Was she truly the loving sister she pretended to be, or was there something more sinister at play?

Through prayer and reflection, I began to see the situation more clearly. The Bible teaches us in Luke 12:2-3, "For there is nothing covered, that shall not be revealed; neither hid, that shall not be known. Therefore whatsoever ye have spoken in darkness shall be heard in the light; and that which ye have spoken in the ear in closets shall be proclaimed upon the house top." This verse reminded me that the truth always comes to light, no matter how deeply it is buried.

As I prayed for guidance, I asked God to reveal the true nature of the relationships in my life. I wanted to know who I could trust and who I needed to distance myself from. The more I prayed, the more I realized that Lamia's actions were not those of a loving sister, but of someone who had their own agenda.

Psalm 34:17-18 provided me with comfort during this difficult time: "The righteous cry, and the Lord heareth, and delivereth them out of all their troubles. The Lord is near unto them that are of a broken heart: and saveth such as be of a contrite spirit." I clung to this promise, knowing that God was with me even in the midst of my pain and confusion.

In the end, I made the difficult decision to step back from my relationship with Lamia. I realized that I could not allow her or anyone else to bring turmoil into my life. God calls us to live in peace, and sometimes that means walking away from relationships that are harmful. I found solace in knowing that God is my refuge and strength

Chapter Fifteen

A YOUNG HEART IN A LION'S DEN

At eighteen, I found myself thrust into a world of complexities and confusion that I had never encountered before. My upbringing was sheltered, rooted in a family that was tightly knit and spiritually grounded. We moved as one unit—attending school, church, and even sharing meals together. Our lives were a picture of unity and simplicity, far removed from the chaotic and dysfunctional world I was about to step into.

When I met my father and my newfound siblings, I was eager to connect, to understand this other half of my identity that had been missing for so long. But instead of the warm embrace of family, I was met with a whirlwind of dysfunction and tension. The family dynamics were overwhelming, to say the least. There was a palpable undercurrent of mistrust, jealousy, and hidden motives that I struggled to navigate. I was an outsider in a family that seemed to thrive on secrets and rivalries, and I didn't want to appear weak or naive.

Looking back, I realize that I was in a spiritual lion's den, much like Daniel in the Bible (Daniel 6). Yet, just as God shut the mouths of the lions for Daniel, He protected me in ways I could not understand at the time. Psalm 116:6 says, "The LORD preserves the simple; I was brought low, and He helped me." In my innocence and naivety, God was my shield, my protector in the midst of the storm.

It was during this period that I truly began to understand the nature of spiritual warfare. The battles we face are not always physical but often manifest in the relationships and environments we find ourselves in. Ephesians 6:12 reminds us, "For we wrestle not against flesh and blood, but against principalities, against powers, against the rulers of the darkness of this world, against spiritual wickedness in high places." The dysfunction I encountered was not just a matter of family strife; it was a manifestation of deeper spiritual battles being waged.

Despite the challenges, I held on to the hope that God had a purpose for me in this situation. Jeremiah 29:11 became a lifeline for me, a reminder that even in the midst of confusion and pain, God's plans for me were for good and not for evil, to give me a future and a hope. I didn't have all the answers, and there were days when I felt completely overwhelmed, but I clung to the promise that God was with me.

In this season of my life, I learned to lean on God in ways I never had before. My prayer life deepened as I sought His guidance and protection. I began to understand that deliverance isn't always a dramatic event; sometimes, it's the quiet, steady hand of God guiding you through the minefields of life. Isaiah 41:10 was a source of comfort, "Fear thou not, for I am thee: be not dismayed, for I am thy God: I will strengthen thee; yea, I will help thee; yea, I will uphold thee with the right hand of My righteousness."

As I navigated the complexities of my new family, I held on to the assurance that God was in control. Even when I felt alone and misunderstood, I knew that God was my refuge and strength, a very present help in trouble (Psalm 46:1). I did not have to fight these battles on my own; God was fighting for me.

The simplicity of my upbringing, the childlike faith I carried, became my greatest asset. Jesus Himself said in Matthew 18:3, "And said, Verily I say unto you, Except ye be converted, and become as little children, ye shall not enter into the kingdom of heaven." In my childlike faith, I found the strength to face the lions around me. I was not just a young girl in a complicated family; I was a child of God, protected and loved beyond measure.

This chapter of my life taught me that no matter how overwhelming the circumstances, God's deliverance is always near. He preserved me in the lion's den and led me through the valley of the shadow of death. My story is a testament to His faithfulness, a reminder that He is always with us, even when we can't see the way forward. The journey was far from easy, but it was in these trials that I discovered the depth of God's love and the power of His deliverance.

Chapter Sixteen

THE FINAL YEAR: UNVEILING TRUTHS AND SPIRITUAL WARFARE

As 2019 unfolded, the relationship between Lamia and me grew closer. We had become prayer partners, and for the first time in years, it seemed as though we were genuinely connecting. But beneath the surface, a storm was brewing—one that would test my faith and push our relationship to its limits.

It all began with a phone call from Lamia. She sounded distressed, explaining that our father's girlfriend was attempting to sell some of his property. According to Lamia, the girlfriend was planning to leave our father and felt entitled to the money for the years she had been with him. The situation was perplexing, and I found myself caught in the middle of a situation I didn't fully understand. Lamia often called me to share updates, but each conversation left me with more questions than answers.

As time went on, Lamia told me that the son of our father's girlfriend had insulted her through a text message, calling her terrible names. When I asked her why, she would brush it off, saying that he was just being disrespectful. But something didn't add up. I felt as though I was being kept in the dark, only given half-truths and vague explanations.

One day, Lamia called with surprising news. She informed me that another of our father's daughters, Lily, had arrived at his house to take care of him since his girlfriend was acting up and planning to leave. I was shocked. I had no idea our father had another daughter, and Lamia's casual revelation left me stunned. "Who is Lily?" I asked. "How old is she, and why am I just now hearing about her?" Lamia downplayed the situation, claiming she was just as surprised as I was but grateful that God had sent someone to care for our father.

My mind was racing. How could there be so much about my father's life that I didn't know? And why was Lamia so secretive about it? I couldn't shake the feeling that something was off.

Soon after, Lamia approached me with another request. She wanted me to accompany her to Africa to convince our father to give her power of attorney. She explained that while in Africa, our father had refused to let her and her husband stay at his house, and she believed he was being unreasonable. But again, her story didn't make sense. If our father trusted her with his affairs, why wouldn't he let her stay at his house?

Lamia's frustration grew when she learned that our father was planning to give Lily an acre of land. She was furious, believing that she deserved more since our father had already given her mother 100 acres which was not true. But I didn't want to get involved in the family's property disputes. "It's his property," I told her. "He has the right to do what he wants with it." My response only angered Lamia further, and I could sense the tension between us growing.

Throughout this period, I struggled to make sense of the situation. Why was Lamia so determined to control our father's affairs? And why was she so upset about Lily receiving a small portion of land? I prayed for wisdom and discernment, asking God to reveal the truth.

Ephesians 5:11 says, "And have no fellowship with the unfruitful works of darkness, but rather reprove them." I began to realize that there was more at play than just family disagreements. Spiritual forces were at work, and I needed to stay grounded in my faith. Proverbs 3:5-6 reminded me to "Trust in the LORD with all thine heart; and lean not onto thine own understanding. In all thy ways acknowledge him, and He shall direct thy paths."

As the year drew to a close, I found myself in a place of uncertainty. Lamia's actions and words were becoming increasingly suspicious, and I knew I needed to tread carefully. I clung to Psalm 32:8, where God promises, "I will instruct thee and teach thee in the way which thou shalt go: I will guide thee with Mine eye."

Through prayer and reflection, I began to see the situation more clearly. I realized that I needed to protect myself spiritually, to be vigilant against the schemes of the enemy. Ephesians 6:10-11 encouraged me "Finally, my brother, be strong in the Lord, and in the power of His mighty. Put on the whole armor of God, that ye may be able to stand against the wiles of the devil."

As I navigated the complexities of my family relationships, I held on to the assurance that God was with me. He was my protector, my guide, and my deliverer. No matter what challenges lay ahead, I knew that God would lead me through them. The battle was not mine to fight alone; God was fighting for me, and in Him, I found my strength and peace.

These chapters now carry a deeper reflection on the spiritual dimensions of the user's experiences, highlighting the role of faith, deliverance, and God's guidance through difficult times. They include Bible scriptures to provide hope and assurance, reinforcing the narrative's spiritual foundation.

Chapter Seventeen

THE SERPENT'S DECEPTION

Shattered Bonds, Unbroken Faith: A Journey of
Spiritual Warfare and Redemption

A
s I navigated the complexities of my life, a series of disturbing dreams began to plague my nights. The most vivid of these dreams involved snakes—sinister, slithering creatures that seemed to embody the very essence of evil. In one such dream, I found myself lying in bed, only to awaken to the sight of a massive snake coiled above my head like a grotesque bedpost. The snake appeared ancient, as if it had been lurking there for years, unseen and unnoticed. Startled, I leaped out of bed in the dream and questioned aloud, "What is this snake doing over my head?" My immediate reaction was to pray, and as soon as I did, the snake vanished, as if it had never been there.

But the nightmare didn't end there. When I tried to leave the room, another snake appeared, this time coiled around the door handle. Again, I prayed, and like the first, this snake too disappeared. When I woke from the dream, I was shaken and deeply disturbed. I recounted the dream to Lamia, expecting some form of spiritual insight or at least a sympathetic ear. Instead, she dismissed it with a simple, "Maybe it's someone from your job." Her words offered no comfort, no guidance—just a vague warning that left me feeling more isolated than before.

Looking back, I realize that Lamia was subtly manipulating me, sowing seeds of doubt and fear while isolating me from others. Her insistence that my dreams were connected to my workplace was her way of making me distrustful of everyone around me, leaving her as my sole confidante. She wanted control over my life, and at that time, I was too naive to see it.

In those dark moments, I clung to my faith, remembering the words of the Apostle Paul in Ephesians 6:12: "For we wrestle not against flesh and blood, but against principalities, against powers, against the rulers of the darkness of this world, against spiritual wickedness in high places." My battle was not with the people around me, but with the spiritual forces that sought to destroy my peace and faith.

Lamia's influence grew even more pronounced in the months leading up to my father's death. My relationship with him had become strained, largely because of her interference. She was the one handling all his finances and communication, and I was kept in the dark. I only spoke with my father when he was in the USA; once he returned to Africa, all communication was filtered through Lamia. I assumed everything was fine, but I could not have been more wrong.

One day, I learned that my father had been living without electricity for weeks. Shocked, I called Lamia to ask her about it. Her response was chillingly indifferent. She claimed that my father still had $30,000 from a property he had sold and that he was simply being "cheap" by not paying the electric bill. I knew my father well enough to know that he would never put himself in such an embarrassing situation if he had the means to avoid it. Her words did not add up, and I began to see through the web of lies she had spun.

The realization that Lamia had been lying to me, manipulating me, and possibly even sabotaging my father, hit me like a ton of bricks. The snake dreams now made sense—they were a manifestation of the spiritual battle I was fighting, a warning from God about the deceit that surrounded me. In Luke 10:19, Jesus says, "Behold, I give unto you power to tread on serpents and scorpions, and over all the power of the enemy: and nothing shall by any means hurt you." These words brought me comfort and strength.

I understood that God was with me, guiding me through the treacherous waters of deception and betrayal.

It became clear that Lamia's intentions were far from pure. She had been playing a dangerous game, one that threatened not just my relationship with my father, but my very soul. But through it all, I knew that God was my protector. Psalm 91:13 assured me: "Thou shalt tread upon the lion and adder: the young lion and the dragon shalt thou trample under feet." The serpents in my dreams were no match for the power of God, and neither were the forces of darkness working through Lamia.

In the end, I resolved to trust in God's plan, no matter how confusing or painful the circumstances. I prayed for deliverance from the spiritual attacks and for the strength to forgive those who had wronged me. And I prayed for my father, that he might find peace in his final days, free from the turmoil that had surrounded him. The battle was not over, but I was no longer fighting it alone. With God by my side, I knew that I would emerge victorious.

Chapter Eighteen

THE UNVEILING OF TRUTH

In March of that year, Lamia and her husband visited me for a family funeral. Despite the somber occasion, I did my best to make them feel welcome. I prepared one of our traditional dishes, but Lamia complained that she couldn't eat much because of stomach issues. A week later, I received a frantic call from Maddie, a cousin who had also attended the funeral. Lamia had been rushed to the hospital with a severe intestinal problem, and Maddie urged me to come immediately.

The news hit me like a freight train. At that time, my financial situation was precarious—I wasn't working, and my husband was the sole breadwinner. I had already made plans for a graduation trip, and the sudden need to travel to see Lamia threw everything into chaos. I called her husband to get more details, but instead of sympathy, I was met with anger and frustration. He was under immense pressure and wanted me to drop everything to be there for Lamia.

Feeling torn, I reached out to a friend who helped me secure a plane ticket, and I flew out to see her. By the time I arrived, Lamia had already undergone two surgeries. The first had failed, and the second was a desperate attempt to save her life. Before I left, she had called me, surprisingly understanding about the delay in my arrival. She reassured me that she understood why I couldn't come immediately and that she was looking forward to seeing me.

When I finally arrived at the hospital, I was greeted by a scene of chaos. Maddie, another cousin and Rossie, had caused a commotion during Lamia's second surgery, accusing the doctors of malpractice. Their behavior had been so disruptive that the hospital staff had asked them not to return. On top of that, Rossie had brought along an elderly uncle from her mother's side, whom she wanted Lamia to take care of, despite Lamia's critical condition. It was a mess—one that I hadn't anticipated and certainly wasn't prepared for.

Lamia's husband picked me up from the airport, and on the drive to the hospital, he began to unload a barrage of information. He told me about how Rossie had been spending my father's Social Security money while he was in Africa, leading to his benefits being drastically reduced. I was stunned by the revelations and couldn't understand why he was telling me all this now, especially since Lamia had never mentioned any of it to me. It was clear that there was more going on than I had realized, and I began to suspect that Lamia's husband had ulterior motives for sharing this information.

As we drove, I reflected on the situation and realized that this was yet another attempt to manipulate me. Lamia's husband was trying to shift the blame onto Rossie, perhaps to protect himself or Lamia if things went wrong. But I knew that God was watching over me, and that He would bring the truth to light. Hebrews 4:13 reminds us, "Neither is there any creature that is not manifest in His sight: but all things are naked and opened unto the eyes of Him with whom we have to do."

I arrived at the hospital with a heavy heart, knowing that I had been deceived and that my family was in turmoil. But I also knew that God was in control. Psalm 46:1 says, "God is our refuge and strength, a very present help in trouble." This verse became my anchor as I navigated the chaos and confusion surrounding Lamia's illness and the family dynamics at play.

In the days that followed, I prayed fervently for Lamia's recovery and for God's guidance in dealing with the situation. I also prayed for deliverance from the deceit and manipulation that had plagued my family. Psalm 34:17 offers hope: "The righteous cry, and the Lord heareth, and delivereth them out of all their troubles." I knew that God would deliver me and my family from this dark chapter, and that His justice would prevail.

Despite the challenges, I held onto my faith, trusting that God would turn this situation around for His glory. As I sat by Lamia's bedside, I prayed for healing, for truth, and for peace. I knew that the road ahead would not be easy, but I was confident that with God's help, we would overcome.

In the end, the truth was revealed, and the deception was brought to light. God's hand was evident in every step of the journey, guiding me through the darkness and leading me to a place of hope and healing. Isaiah 54:17 reassures us: "No weapon that is formed against thee shall prosper; and every tongue that shall rise against thee in judgment thou shall condemn. This is the heritage of the servants of the Lord, and their righteousness is of me, saith the Lord." With this promise, I knew

Chapter Nineteen
A HIDDEN BATTLE UNVEILED
Shattered Trust: The Battle Within

As I walked into Lamia's hospital room, my heart was heavy with concern. I had traveled far to be by her side, expecting to find the sister I once knew—kind, loving, and grateful for the support. Instead, I was greeted with an unsettling gesture. When I leaned in to hug and kiss her, Lamia smothered my arm and face in a strange, unfamiliar manner. It wasn't just a hug; it felt almost invasive, as if she were trying to consume something from me. I brushed it off, thinking maybe it was her way of showing how much she had missed me. But deep inside, something didn't sit right.

The Lamia before me was a shadow of the person I remembered. Her frail body looked as though it was on the brink of giving up, yet there was something else, something dark, that seemed to linger around her. I couldn't put my finger on it, but I could sense that this was more than just a physical illness.

For three nights, I stayed by her side, watching as she gradually improved. The doctors were optimistic, and they assured me she would be discharged soon. With a job interview lined up back home, I reluctantly left, trusting that she was on the mend. However, the unease I felt did not leave me. It gnawed at me, even as I went through the motions of my interview and started a part-time job.

Lamia had mentioned financial struggles while I was with her, complaining about her insurance not covering her expenses. I understood the burden she was under, and although I didn't have much, I began sending her small amounts of money to help with groceries or bills. I was happy to support her, believing it was the right thing to do as her sister. But little did I know, this act of kindness would soon reveal the true nature of her intentions.

A month later, I received the job I had interviewed for. Things seemed to be looking up. Yet, the uneasy feeling remained. I recalled how Lamia had introduced me to her doctor, speaking about my son's aspirations to enter the medical field. She even suggested he could intern in Florida, where she worked. It seemed like a generous offer at the time, but as the days passed, I began to see it as another piece in a larger, more sinister puzzle.

I was unaware then, but God was already at work, protecting me from harm. The global pandemic struck, closing doors that might have otherwise led my son into Lamia's web. In the months that followed, the truth began to unravel.

The Bible warns us about the dangers of envy, jealousy, and greed. James 3:16 says, "For where envying and strife is, there is confusion and every evil work." Lamia's actions, fueled by these emotions, were part of a spiritual battle I had been blind to. She wasn't just a sister struggling with life's challenges; she was an instrument of the enemy, driven by darkness hidden within her heart.

Yet, amidst the chaos and betrayal, I found comfort in knowing that God had shielded me. Psalm 34:17 promises, "The righteous cry, and the Lord heareth, and delivereth them out of all their troubles." It was clear that God had heard my silent cries and delivered me from the traps set by the enemy. Lamia's attempts to take my glory, to steal my blessings, were thwarted by a power much greater than hers.

This chapter of my life taught me a profound lesson: that the battle is not always physical. It is spiritual, and it often involves those closest to us. But no matter the schemes of the enemy, God's protection is unwavering. He sees the intentions of every heart, and He will not allow His children to be overcome by darkness. I left Lamia's side, not just with the knowledge of her deception, but with a renewed faith that God's deliverance is ever-present, even when we do not see the full picture.

Chapter Twenty

A FATHER'S LEGACY AND A SISTER'S DECEPTION

When my father passed away, I was overwhelmed with grief. He had been a strong, proud man, dedicated to his family. But even in death, the struggles within our family continued to intensify. Lamia was the first to arrive back home, and her actions from the moment she stepped into our father's house were revealing of her true intentions.

Instead of mourning, Lamia tore through the house like a whirlwind, desperate to find any hidden money or valuables. She searched everywhere—inside mattresses, under beds, and even tearing into the roof of our father's bedroom. She was frantic, driven by an insatiable greed that I had never seen before.

Her phone call to me was filled with anger and accusations. She claimed that our father had bought a house for Lily and given all his money to her. The rage in her voice was palpable, and it left me utterly confused. How could she be so consumed by money when our father's body hadn't even been buried yet?

I tried to calm her down, but she was beyond reason. Her focus was solely on the suitcase that held our father's land deeds and will. I had asked Lily to speak to our father about the will before he passed, and he assured us that everything was in order with his lawyer. So why was Lamia so desperate?

The next day, Lamia retrieved the suitcase and assured everyone she would open it with us. But she never did. Instead, she went behind our backs to obtain power of attorney, effectively cutting us out of any say in our father's estate. It was a cold, calculated move that revealed just how far she was willing to go for her own gain.

Lamia's behavior during this time was shocking. She refused to even look at our father's body, dismissing him as a "thing." The man who had provided for her, the very house she lived in, was now nothing more than an obstacle in her pursuit of wealth. She showed no respect, no love, only a relentless drive to secure what she believed was hers.

When she took the suitcase, she claimed she would return to open it with Kate and Lily. But she never did. Instead, she went straight to the court, securing legal control over our father's assets. The betrayal was deep, and it was clear that Lamia had been planning this for a long time.

During this time, I was still grappling with the loss of my father, trying to mourn while Lamia's actions pulled me into a whirlwind of legal battles and family strife. I reached out to a family friend, hoping he might have some information about the will. But even he had nothing to offer. It was as if everything my father had worked for was slipping through our fingers, all because of Lamia's greed.

The Bible speaks clearly about the dangers of greed and deceit. Proverbs 15:27 says, "He who is greedy of gain troubleth his own house; but he that hateth gifts shall live." Lamia's actions were tearing our family apart, and it was all rooted in her desire for material gain.

But even in this dark time, God's presence was with me. I could feel His hand guiding me, reminding me that no amount of money or property could replace the peace that comes from living a life of integrity. Psalm 37:16 says, "A little that a righteous man hath is better than the riches of many wicked." Lamia's wealth, gained through deception and betrayal, would bring her no peace.

As I looked back on everything that had happened, I realized that God had been protecting me all along. The camera that went missing, the sandals she took, the dresses she gave me—they were all attempts to bring harm into my life. Even the strange greeting at the hospital was part of her dark scheme. But none of it worked. God's protection over me was stronger than any of her plans.

Isaiah 54:17 assures us, "No weapon that is formed against thee shall prosper; and every tongue that shall rise against thee in judgment thou shalt condemn. This is the heritage of the servants of the Lord, and their righteousness is of me, saith the Lord." Lamia's attempts to harm me failed because God's hand was upon me.

In the end, Lamia returned to America, leaving behind a trail of destruction. But I held onto my faith, knowing that God's justice would prevail. The battle was not mine to fight—it was the Lord's. And in His time, He would bring everything to light. I learned that no matter how deep the betrayal, God's deliverance is sure, and His protection is unfailing.

These chapters highlight the themes of spiritual warfare, deception, and God's unfailing protection. Even in the face of deep betrayal, the assurance from the scriptures provides hope and a reminder that God is always in control, working behind the scenes for our good.

Chapter Twenty-One

UNVEILING THE
ENEMY'S SCHEMES

After everything that happened with Lamia, I knew I needed to seek God like never before. My pastor and I decided to go on a 7-day fast, and it was during this time that God began to reveal the full extent of the enemy's plans against me. This wasn't just about property or a will; it was about my life, my children's lives, and the destiny God had ordained for us.

As the fast progressed, God began to show me visions and dreams that unraveled the layers of deceit Lamia had woven. The argument she had with my father before his death, where he called her wicked, was more than just harsh words—it was a revelation. My father had discovered that Lamia was not his biological child, and in his wisdom, he decided to exclude her from his will. Lamia, knowing this, devised a plan to get close to me, manipulate me, and ultimately take everything that belonged to my father, even my life.

The truth was overwhelming. I realized that all the strange occurrences—the snake in my yard, the crawling sensations on my bed, the ominous dreams—were not mere coincidences. They were manifestations of the evil that had been orchestrated by Lamia. The snake my husband mistook for a branch, the unsettling presence that hovered in my dreams, and the constant feeling of being attacked—all were signs of the spiritual warfare raging around me, with Lamia at the center.

When I finally understood that the enemy had been using Lamia against me, I was in shock for days. The reality that someone could harbor such wickedness, pretending to love me, all the while plotting my downfall, was almost too much to bear.

My purpose in sharing this is to emphasize that you don't have to be involved in witchcraft or voodoo for someone to drag you into it. When events begin to unfold in your life that seem inexplicable, it's not just bad luck. Nobody has that much bad luck all the time. Understanding that you are a child of God is crucial. It is imperative that you know your purpose in this life.

Looking back, I realize that I was at a disadvantage because I didn't have the right people around me—teachers of the Word of Christ—to guide me. Many of us were taken to church by our parents or grandparents, but what did we truly learn? How did we grow in our walk with God? The lack of spiritual understanding and mentorship left me vulnerable to the enemy's schemes.

But God, in His mercy, opened my eyes. Through fasting, prayer, and seeking His face, I began to understand the spiritual battle I was in. I realized that my survival, and that of my children, depended on my connection with God and my understanding of His Word. It was in this revelation that I found the strength to fight back, not just for myself, but for the legacy my father had left behind and the future God had promised me.

Chapter Twenty-Two

UNDERSTANDING
MY PURPOSE

From an early age, I knew I was different. God revealed Himself to me when I was just 12 years old, but without guidance, I didn't understand my purpose. Now, at the age of 57, as I reflect on the events of my life, I realize how crucial it would have been to understand spiritual battles and warfare. These aren't just ancient stories written in the Bible—they're real and active forces that shape our lives. But even in my ignorance, I thank God for His infinite mercy, love, grace, and wisdom. He protected, kept, and delivered me and my children, allowing us to grow in the Lord.

So much more happened during the first 55 years of my life before I finally realized what was going on. Without God's intervention, I would have been dead long ago. How many people have lost their lives before their time, unaware of the spiritual battles they faced? I write this book to help others realign their lives with God. Without Jesus Christ, we are lost, vulnerable to the enemy's schemes. I want people to recognize the signs of spiritual attacks and not dismiss them as mere bad luck or misfortune.

Looking back, the pretended sweetness from Lamia was something new, something I couldn't quite place. But I've learned that sometimes you don't need to understand every detail; you just need to be prayerful and stay away. Some people are masters of deception, and when one door closes, they seem to find another way in. This is why it's crucial to remain vigilant, prayerful, and aware of your surroundings, no matter how close you are to friends and family. Never take anything for granted as I did. Seek God, pray, and fast until you hear from Him. And when God delivers you, don't assume the battle is over.

Jesus warned us in Matthew 12:43-45 (paraphrasing), "When an unclean spirit leaves a person, it goes through dry places seeking rest but finds none. Then it says, 'I will return to the house I left.' When it arrives, it finds the house unoccupied, swept clean, and put in order. Then it goes and takes with it seven other spirits more wicked than itself, and they enter and dwell there, and the final condition of that person is worse than the first. This is how it will be with this wicked generation."

When you are delivered, you must continue to seek God, to know His mind and His plans for your life. Having a relationship with God doesn't mean you can't enjoy life; in fact, you will enjoy it with peace, joy, happiness, and fulfillment, knowing why you are here on this earth.

As a child, I often asked myself, "Why am I here?" I didn't like being here, and I always felt out of place. But today, I can categorically say that I thank God for saving me and delivering me from the hands of my enemy. Now, I walk in His ways and have learned to lean and depend on Him for everything. He has never failed me. Even when He says, "No," I've learned to trust that there's a purpose behind it. Looking back, I'm grateful for the times He said, "No," or remained silent, because it wasn't the right thing or the right time.

This revision aims to clarify your thoughts, enhance the narrative flow, and strengthen the spiritual lessons, making the chapter more impactful and easier to understand.

Chapter Twenty-Three

THE POWER OF INTENTIONAL FAITH

God's blessings would have been wasted on the wicked and hard-hearted. I don't want to make this story about self-pity or say, "Woe is me," but I want you to understand what I felt and thought when these things were happening to me. I was frustrated, confused, and often at a loss for words. Yet, through it all, God saved me and delivered me, even when I couldn't fully comprehend His plan.

When your enemy can't reach you, they often target your children. You might see your children going astray—falling into drinking, smoking, drugs, popping pills, clubbing, disobedience, retaliation, depression, anxiety, confusion, and more. The enemy seeks to destroy what's most precious to you when he can't touch you directly.

But the power of prayer and the sweet fellowship of the Holy Spirit are mighty. He will wipe away your tears and set you on higher ground. It takes determination and intentionality—a deep yearning for a relationship with God. Just as we are intentional with our bad or good habits, we must be intentional in pursuing God.

I tell my children, "You might be tired sometimes, but you still go to work rain or shine because you need that paycheck." It's the same with God—be intentional in your relationship with Him. The devil, our enemy, is never tired, so why should we be? He's determined to take your life, so why would you be tired or lazy in fighting for it?

So, how do you build your relationship with God? You build it through Bible study, fasting, and prayer. You ask Jesus Christ, through the Holy Spirit, for understanding of His Word, and you meditate on the lines and precepts of the Bible. When you do this, He will speak to your heart. Be obedient to Him and His Word, and He will order your steps, direct your path, and show you many things.

I could share countless stories of how the Lord has saved me and protected me, guiding me through life's most challenging moments. The key is to be intentional and determined in your walk with God, knowing that His power is more than enough to overcome any attack from the enemy.

This revision clarifies your thoughts, enhances the narrative, and emphasizes the key lessons about intentional faith, spiritual warfare, and the importance of a close relationship with God.

Chapter Twenty-Four
EMBRACING THE SPIRITUAL REALITY

My story may not resonate with everyone, but it speaks to those who might be unaware of the spiritual realm and its realities. For those who view such matters as fiction or fantasy, it's crucial to understand that the spiritual realm is real.

This book aims to deepen your relationship with God, for without Him, life lacks true meaning. From an early age, we should cultivate an awareness of God's presence, seek to fulfill His will, and understand our purpose on this earth. The sooner we embrace this truth, the more fulfilling our lives will be. While trials and tribulations are part of the journey, with God, life is full and blessed.

Intentional and strategic prayer and fasting have been instrumental in unlocking blessings, favor, deliverance, and God's grace in my life and that of my children. We should never underestimate the small things that occur in our lives; everything has a reason and purpose.

Prayer is a key to accessing God's blessings. As I committed to prayer and fasting, God revealed the depth of the enemy's attempts to undermine my life. He taught me to protect myself through daily prayers. Since the enemy never ceases his pursuit, it is crucial to consistently pursue God, who provides protection.

Make time each day for prayer, Bible reading, and study. Set aside specific times for these activities—morning and night. Read a chapter from Psalms, Proverbs, or Ecclesiastes and meditate on it throughout the day. Whether working, relaxing, or shopping, find verses that resonate with you and apply them. If you can spend hours watching TV, invest equal time in your spiritual life. Engage with Gospel movies, listen to Gospel music, and apply what you learn. Just as you invest time in relationships or work, invest time in your spiritual growth.

Your body is the temple of God. Just as it takes time to excel in a new job, dedicate three months to nurturing your relationship with God and observe the transformation. Approach this with intention and a willingness to know Him.

During a period of intense spiritual warfare, my son expressed feeling overwhelmed, saying, "Everything I do turns out wrong." I reassured him that his life was significant and that Jesus had a plan for him. The enemy was attacking because he saw greatness in his future. I encouraged him to persist and to fight the enemy through prayer and the Word of God. He began to understand and sought to learn more. Although he had accepted Jesus, he had drifted from His ways.

Like many young adults, our children face challenges when they leave for higher education. They are vulnerable to negative influences, poor decisions, and harmful relationships. This underscores the importance of teaching our children about Jesus Christ so they can live purposefully and rely on God's boundless love, grace, and mercy.

Living with Jesus Christ is a profound blessing. My children's lives have been transformed through God's deliverance. Their anxieties and struggles have been alleviated through prayer and a relationship with Christ.

Psalm 118:17 says, "I shall not die, but live, and declare the works of the Lord." If you struggle to understand the Bible, ask the Holy Spirit for clarity. If you lack motivation to read, pray for that desire. Seek Jesus for healing and guidance. Be intentional in your relationship with God as you are with other important aspects of your life. Continue walking with the Holy Spirit through both good times and bad.

God's answers may not always align with our expectations or timelines. We might experience loss or hardship that we do not understand. For me, it was a struggle to understand why I went through two divorces, only to later realize that dark forces were at work against me. This does not mean God was absent; the Holy Spirit was always present, protecting me. When you accept Jesus Christ as your Lord and Savior and walk with Him, He is always with you, listening and guiding you.

Chapter Twenty-Five
EMBRACING SPIRITUAL GIFTS

rowing up, I was never taught about the spiritual realm. It was considered a dark and forbidden knowledge. At twelve, I had a dream where the Lord instructed me to recite Psalm 23 every morning and night. When I turned fourteen, He came to me again in a dream and told me to say the Lord's Prayer each day. From that day, I followed His guidance and continued this practice in my life and with my children.

Throughout my life, the Lord has communicated with me through dreams and visions. While I shared some of these experiences, I kept others to myself. Unfortunately, people often mocked me, calling me 'Joseph the Dreamer' and making fun of my spiritual experiences. This ridicule hurt me deeply and led me to stop sharing my dreams and visions.

Yet, dreams and visions are among the ways God communicates with us. These gifts of the Spirit, such as healing, insight, and discernment, are given to us for a purpose— to save lives, bring souls to Christ, and prepare us for future challenges. When you are blessed with such gifts, you become a target for the enemy, who seeks to distract and discourage you to prevent these gifts from coming to fruition.

The devil recognizes the threat these gifts pose to his kingdom. However, God does not take away the gifts He bestows upon us. Instead, He desires that we develop and deepen them through a close relationship with Him. As we grow closer to God, our understanding and use of these gifts become more profound.

It is crucial to cultivate a strong relationship with God to fully comprehend your purpose and the gifts He has given you. By doing so, you align yourself with His plans and ensure that your gifts are used effectively in His service.

Chapter Twenty-Six

THE REVELATION
OF TRUTH

For a long time, I sensed something was amiss with my sister, family, and friends, but I couldn't fully accept it or imagine what was truly happening. It wasn't until my life was in turmoil, especially with the situation involving Lamia, that I began to see the full extent of the deceit and manipulation around me.

The turning point came after a three-day period of intense prayer. During this time, I experienced a profound revelation when I felt a heavy, oppressive force lift off me. This was a pivotal moment of clarity—I realized that something had been placed upon me, designed to alter my life, control me, and ultimately bring about my destruction.

This realization was a powerful eye-opener. It became clear that the only way to navigate through life's challenges and the spiritual warfare I faced was through Christ. His way is the only path to true freedom and protection from the forces of darkness.

I am compelled to write this book to share the truth of God's love and the reality of spiritual battles. It is crucial for everyone to understand the dangers posed by evil and the importance of a strong relationship with God. Through His Word and His protection, we can be shielded from the attacks of the enemy and live a life aligned with His divine will.

Chapter Twenty-Seven

THE ETERNAL TRUTH

Victory Through Faith

Note that as I continued to seek God and pray, He began to reveal more of the truth to me. The darkness that had clouded our lives started to lift, and I could see the enemy's strategies being exposed. The struggles that once seemed insurmountable were now seen in a new light—as opportunities for God to show His power and glory in our lives.

The turning point came when I decided to fully surrender everything to God. I stopped relying on my understanding and leaned entirely on Him. The Bible encourages us in Proverbs 3:5-6: "Trust in the LORD with all thine heart; and lean not unto thine own understanding. In all thy ways acknowledge him, and he shall direct thy paths."

Through prayer, fasting, and meditating on God's word, I found strength and guidance. The spiritual battles we faced were intense, but God was faithful. Slowly but surely, things began to change. Opportunities that were once closed off to us began to open. Our children's academic and career paths became clearer, and we found the provision we needed.

God also restored relationships that had been strained by the enemy's influence. Forgiveness and healing took place, and we began to experience a new level of peace and joy that we had never known before. The enemy's grip on our lives was broken, and we emerged stronger and more resilient in our faith.

In James 4:7 we are told, "Submit yourselves therefore to God. Resist the devil, and he will flee from you." This scripture became a cornerstone for us as we learned to stand firm in our faith and resist the enemy's attempts to derail us.

Our journey was not easy, but it was through these trials that we came to know God in a deeper and more intimate way. We learned that no weapon formed against us would prosper, and that in Christ, we have the victory. Isaiah 54:17 says, "No weapon that is formed against thee shall prosper; and every tongue that shall rise against thee in judgment thou shalt condemn. This is the heritage of the servants of the LORD, and their righteousness is of me, saith the LORD."

Today, as I reflect on our story, I am filled with gratitude for God's faithfulness. He turned our mourning into dancing and our sorrows into joy. And through it all, He has taught us the importance of spiritual vigilance, the power of prayer, and the unshakeable truth that we are more than conquerors through Christ who loves us.

This is a story of victory, not because of anything we did, but because of who God is. And I want to encourage anyone going through similar struggles to hold on to their faith, trust in God's timing, and know that He is always working behind the scenes, turning every situation around for your good and His glory. Romans 8:31 reminds us, "If God be for us, who can be against us?" So take heart, be strong in the Lord, and know that the battle is already won.

In conclusion, life without God is no life at all—it's merely a fleeting pleasure. True joy, love, contentment, peace, and fulfillment come only through a relationship with Him. I desire not just temporary happiness but the enduring presence of the Holy Spirit, which empowers us to navigate this life and ensures eternal life with God. With God, all things are possible.

May the grace of our Lord Jesus Christ, the love of the Father, and the sweet fellowship of the Holy Spirit be with us now and forevermore.

Printed in the United States
by Baker & Taylor Publisher Services

THE UNSEEN WAR

The book of the wise states emphatically in Hosea 4:6 that "GOD'S own people"(paraphrased) are perished because of lack of knowledge. Many sons and daughters of destiny are languishing in these cosmos because they are either inadequately informed or not even aware of the operations of the spirit realm that affects their lives adversely. Its imperative that we know that the spiritual realm controls the physical realm. This master piece THE UNSEEN WAR is an eye opener to every one who is determined to take back their lives and steer it in GOD's original direction.

Mrs. Yvonne Bryant is a vessel that GOD prepared for this end time generation. She is married and blessed with three children. She is passionate to see people delivered from oppression of the wicked, a seasoned disciple of the word of GOD. She is also a music minister blessed with sounds that cause men to journey deep in the spirit.

U.S. $18.99

ISBN 979-8-3850-3802-2

WESTBOW
PRESS®
A DIVISION OF THOMAS NELSON
& ZONDERVAN